RANGE
PAINTED TURTLE

RANGE
RED-EARED SLIDER
TURTLE

RANGE
BOX TURTLE

RANGE
ALABAMA RED-BELLIED
TURTLE

RANGE
MOJAVE DESERT
TORTOISE

RANGE
BLANDING'S TURTLE

CANADA

UNITED STATES of AMERICA

MEXICO

OF AMERICA

UNITED STATES

MEXICO

NADA

STATES OF AMERICA

A PLACE FOR
TURTLES

For Gerard
—M. S.

For my precious turtledove,
Annabella Patrycja Bond
—H. B.

PEACHTREE PUBLISHERS
1700 Chattahoochee Avenue
Atlanta, Georgia 30318-2112
www.peachtree-online.com

Text © 2013, 2019 by Melissa Stewart
Illustrations © 2013, 2019 by Higgins Bond

Edited by Vicky Holifield
Book design by Loraine M. Joyner
Composition by Adela Pons
Illustrations created in acrylic on cold press illustration board

Printed in October 2018 by Tien Wah Press in Malaysia
10 9 8 7 6 5 4 3 2 1 (hardcover)
10 9 8 7 6 5 4 3 2 1 (trade paperback)
Revised Edition

HC ISBN: 978-1-68263-096-9
PB ISBN: 978-1-68263-097-6

Library of Congress Cataloging-in-Publication Data
Stewart, Melissa.
A place for turtles / written by Melissa Stewart ; illustrated by Higgins
Bond.
pages cm
Includes bibliographical references.
Audience: Age 4-8.
ISBN 978-1-56145-693-2 / 1-56145-693-4
1. Turtles—Juvenile literature. 2. Rare reptiles—Juvenile literature. 3.
Turtles—Conservation—Juvenile literature. I. Bond, Higgins, illustrator. II.
Title.
QL666.C5S83 2013
597.92—dc23
2012025538

A PLACE FOR
TURTLES

Written by
Melissa Stewart

Illustrated by
Higgins Bond

PEACHTREE
ATLANTA

Turtles make our world a better place. But sometimes people do things that make it hard for them to live and grow.

If we work together to help these special creatures, there will always be a place for turtles.

A LOOK AT TURTLES

Turtles are closely related to snakes, lizards, and crocodiles. They all belong to a group of animals called reptiles. Some turtles spend most of their lives on land. Other turtles live in lakes, rivers, or the ocean. But all turtles hatch from tough leathery eggs laid on land. Young turtles are tiny, but they look just like their parents.

spotted turtle

Like all living things, turtles need safe places to raise their young. Some turtles have trouble building nests when new kinds of plants spread into their home habitat.

When people find ways to control the new plants, turtles can live and grow.

BOG TURTLE

Because purple loosestrife has pretty purple flowers and can be used as a medicine, European settlers brought the plant to North America. But when thick clusters of loosestrife began growing in wetlands, bog turtles couldn't find sunny spots for their nests. Today scientists in twenty-seven states use beetles to control loosestrife. The insects eat loosestrife leaves, causing the plants to die. That means bog turtles now have plenty of places to build their nests.

Young turtles don't stand a chance when people add fish to lakes and ponds.

WESTERN POND TURTLE

As Americans moved west in the 1800s, they added largemouth bass to the lakes and ponds near their new homes. These fish devoured tiny turtle hatchlings. By the mid-1990s, almost all of Washington State's western pond turtles were gone.

When scientists noticed the problem, they asked people to help them collect hatchlings. The young turtles are raised at zoos until they're big enough to survive in the wild. Thanks to this program, the western pond turtle population is now growing in Washington.

When people collect newly-hatched turtles and raise them in safe places, turtles can live and grow.

Adult turtles face many dangers too. Some sea turtles die when they're accidentally caught by fishing equipment.

When fishing crews make changes to their gear and the way they do their work, turtles can live and grow.

LOGGERHEAD TURTLE

In the past, huge numbers of loggerhead turtles died in nets used to catch shrimp. Then, in 1988, fishing crews began using nets with escape hatches for sea turtles. This helped loggerheads, but many were still hooked on fishing lines set out for swordfish and tuna. Others were trapped by equipment used to catch crabs and scallops.

In 2011, the U.S. government passed a law protecting loggerheads. Now researchers are developing more turtle-friendly fishing gear. Scientists close fishing areas when turtles are passing through. Hopefully, loggerheads can make a comeback.

Because plastic shopping bags look like jellyfish, sea turtles sometimes eat them by mistake. The plastic can clog the turtle's stomach, causing it to starve to death.

LEATHERBACK TURTLE

In the mid-1980s, stores across North America switched from paper shopping bags to plastic ones. Because plastic never breaks down, millions of shopping bags have ended up in the ocean where they can harm leatherback turtles. Today many families bring their own reusable cloth bags to the grocery store. Small changes like this can help save sea turtles.

When people stop using plastic shopping bags, turtles can live
and grow.

Some turtles taste so delicious that people eat too many of them.

When lawmakers stop people from hunting the tasty reptiles,
turtles can live and grow.

DIAMONDBACK TERRAPIN

In the late 1800s, people in Maryland and Virginia caught close to 100,000 diamondback terrapins every year. They used the meat to make turtle soup. By the 1920s, the terrapins were almost all gone. Fancy restaurants stopped serving turtle soup, but some people kept eating the meat. Today, the turtles are protected in most of the states where they live. But they're still struggling to survive.

Many people let their dogs run free when they go hiking in natural areas. But curious dogs can injure turtles and other small animals.

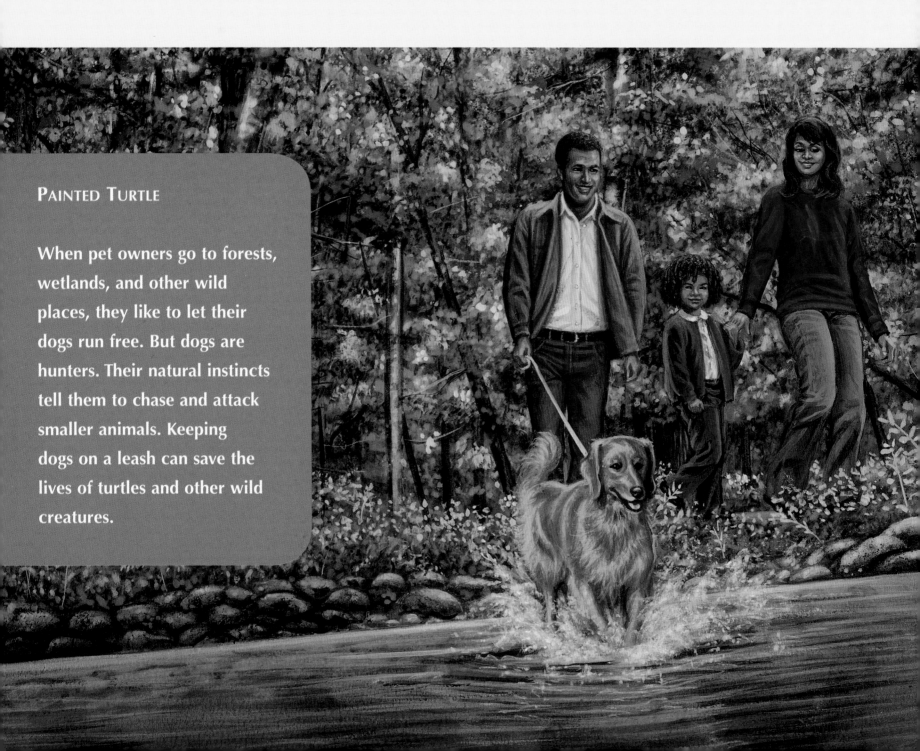

PAINTED TURTLE

When pet owners go to forests, wetlands, and other wild places, they like to let their dogs run free. But dogs are hunters. Their natural instincts tell them to chase and attack smaller animals. Keeping dogs on a leash can save the lives of turtles and other wild creatures.

When hikers keep their dogs on leashes, turtles can live and grow.

Some turtles have such colorful bodies and shells that people like to keep them as pets.

When people stop collecting these beautiful reptiles,
turtles can live and grow.

RED-EARED SLIDER TURTLE

Red-eared slider turtles have colorful bodies and interesting shells, so some people are tempted to take them home. But a turtle is a wild animal. It can't form a special bond with people, and living in a terrarium is stressful. It's against the law to catch or sell young turtles, but it's best to let all turtles—even the older ones—live in their natural habitats.

Many people think it's fun to watch turtle races at fairs, picnics, and rodeos. But when turtles from different places come into contact with one another, they can get sick.

When people learn the truth about these races and stop them, turtles can live and grow.

BOX TURTLE

Each year, people catch thousands of box turtles and enter them in races. During a race, turtles may pass germs to one another. Many turtles get sick and die after a race. Even if the turtles stay healthy, people may not return them to their original homes. That makes it hard for the turtles to survive. Racing turtles may seem like fun, but turtles are better off when we leave them alone.

Turtles have dark bodies, and they move slowly. People driving cars may not see them—until it's too late.

ALABAMA RED-BELLIED TURTLE

Alabama red-bellied turtles face many dangers. Between 2001 and 2006, more than 400 were killed trying to cross a four-lane highway called the Mobile Causeway. In 2007, workers built a fence, so turtles couldn't wander onto the road. Did the fence work? Yes! According to scientists, many turtle lives have been saved.

Alabama red-bellied turtle

When people build turtle-proof fences along busy highways,
turtles can live and grow.

Turtles have trouble surviving when their natural homes are destroyed. Some turtles can only live in sandy deserts with lots of shrubs.

When people protect these natural places, turtles can live and grow.

MOJAVE DESERT TORTOISE

In the 1950s, Las Vegas, Nevada, became a popular place to live. As the city grew, workers built homes, businesses, and parking lots on the land where Mojave desert tortoises lived. Soon the turtles were in trouble. In 1990, the U. S. Fish and Wildlife Service added the tortoises to the threatened species list. Now people are working hard to protect the desert areas where the turtles live.

Other turtles can only survive in shallow marshes and ponds.

BLANDING'S TURTLE

In 1996, LaGrange, New York, needed to make their high school larger. But the only place to expand was a wetland where Blanding's turtles lived. To solve the problem, workers moved soil and plants to create a new home for the turtles. In 2014, people made changes to the land at a nearby park so the turtles will have even more places to live. Scientists hope the turtles will thrive in their new surroundings.

Blanding's turtle

When people create new wetlands, turtles can live and grow.

When too many turtles die, other living things may also have trouble surviving.

That's why it's so important to protect turtles and the places where they live.

OTHER ANIMALS NEED TURTLES

Turtles are an important part of animal food chains. Turtle eggs are good sources of food for snakes, lizards, otters, raccoons, badgers, rats, herons, and gulls. Adult turtles are eaten by coyotes, foxes, weasels, minks, skunks, opossums, eagles, osprey, alligators, crocodiles, and sharks. Without a thriving population of turtles, many other creatures would go hungry.

Turtles have lived on Earth for more than 220 million years.

Sometimes people do things that can harm turtles. But there are many ways you can help these special creatures live far into the future.

HELPING TURTLES

❖ **Don't catch and keep turtles.** Let them live in their natural environment.

❖ **Don't buy turtles at a pet store.** Turtles are wild animals and should live in their natural homes.

❖ **If someone gives you a turtle, don't release it in a wild place.** It could make other turtles sick.

❖ **Don't throw trash into a body of water or pour household cleaners or other chemicals down the drain.**

❖ **Join a group of people working to protect or restore rivers, lakes, streams, ponds, or ocean areas near your home.**

❖ **May 23 is World Turtle Day.** Don't forget to shell-ebrate!

Turtle Facts

* No one knows how many kinds of turtles live on Earth. So far, scientists have discovered more than 350 different species. About seventy kinds of turtles live in North America.

* The bog turtle is the smallest turtle on Earth. It is just 4 inches long. The leatherback turtle is the world's largest turtle. It can grow more than 6 feet long and weigh as much as an elephant.

bog turtle

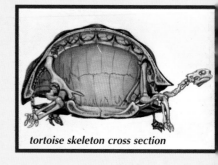

tortoise skeleton cross section

* A turtle's shell is made up of sixty different bones.

* Most land turtles, like box turtles and desert tortoises, have high, domed shells. Turtles that live in rivers, lakes, or the ocean have low, flat shells.

* Some turtles can live more than 100 years. A few species can survive more than a year without food.

Selected Sources

"Blanding's Turtle: Habitat Restoration Project," Hudsonia: A Non-profit Environmental Research Institute. www.hudsonia.org/programs/conservation-ecology/blandings-turtle.

Ernst, Carl, and Jeffrey Lovich. *Turtles of the United States and Canada.* Baltimore, MD: Johns Hopkins University Press, 2009.

"James Baird State Park Golf Course Gets $3.2 Million Upgrade, Protects Endangered Turtles," *Mid-Hudson News,* September 29, 2014. www.midhudsonnews.com/News/2014/September/29/BairdGC_grant-29Sep14.html.

"Loggerhead Turtle *(Caretta caretta)*" NOAA Fisheries, February 22, 2017. www.fisheries.noaa.gov/species/loggerhead-turtle.

"New Jersey Bog Turtle Project." New Jersey Division of Fish and Wildlife. www.state.nj.us/dep/fgw/bogturt.htm.

Potts, Haley. "Red-bellied Turtle," *Mobile Bay,* August 2014. www.mobilebaymag.com/natural-selections-pseudemys-alabamensis/.

"Purple Loosestrife Control: Biological," Minnesota Department of Natural Resources. www.dnr.state.mn.us/invasives/aquaticplants/purpleloosestrife/biocontrol.html.

"Saving Blanding's Turtles," TeacherTube video created by students at Arlington High School, LaGrange, NY. www.teachertube.com/viewVideo.php?video_id=167497&title=Blandings_Turtle.

"Status of the Desert Tortoise in Its Critical Habitat," U.S. Fish and Wildlife Service, October, 2017. www.fws.gov/nevada/desert_tortoise/documents/misc/status-desert-tortoise.pdf.

"Western Pond Turtles in Washington," Washington Department of Fish & Wildlife, February 2014. www.wdfw.wa.gov/conservation/western_pond_turtle.

Recommended for Young Readers

Chiang, Mona. "The Plight of the Turtle." *Science World.* May 9, 2003, pp. 8–14.

Davies, Nicola. *One Tiny Turtle.* Cambridge, MA: Candlewick, 2005.

"Don't Take the Turtles." *Boy's Quest.* April–May 2003, pp. 20–21.

Marsh, Laura. *Sea Turtles.* Washington, D.C.: National Geographic for Kids, 2011.

Sayre, April Pulley. *Turtle, Turtle, Watch Out!* Watertown, MA: Charlesbridge, 2010.

Winner, Cherie. *Everything Reptile: What Kids Really Want to Know About Reptiles.* Minnetonka, MN: NorthWord Books for Young Readers, 2004.

Acknowledgments

The author wishes to thank Andrea Beshara, a turtle research biologist who serves as a naturalist instructor and education animal coordinator at the Oklahoma City Zoo in Oklahoma City, Oklahoma, for her help in preparing this manuscript.

Galapagos tortoise

OF AMERICA

☐ RANGE
SPOTTED TURTLE

AMERICA

☐ RANGE
BOG TURTLE

UNITED STATES

☐ RANGE
WESTERN POND
TURTLE

☐ RANGE
LOGGERHEAD
TURTLE

☐ RANGE
LEATHERBACK
TURTLE

D A

☐ RANGE
DIAMONDBACK
TERRAPIN

CANADA

UNITED STATES OF AMERICA

CANADA

UNITED STATES OF AMERICA

MEXICO

S OF AMERICA

All range boundaries are approximate.